1

MERRY
CHRISTMAS!

2

Merry &
BRIGHT

3

4

5

6

7

8

9

10

have
yourself
a
merry
LITTLE
Christmas

11

Christmas
Cheer

12

13

14

MERRY
CHRISTMAS

15

16

BABY
it's
COLD
outside

17

18

don't
Get your
tinsel
in a
Tangle

19

20

eat
drink
& BE
merry

21

22

have
A
holly jolly
Christmas

23

24

Made in the USA
Monee, IL
24 November 2024

71057309R00031